Something Fishy

by Barry Louis Polisar

illustrations by David Clark

Sweetlips Fish

An odd name for a fish,
And perhaps a bit explicit.

It might be a sweetlips fish,
But I would never kiss it.

Amoeba

An amoeba is as basic as
An animal can get,
With qualities suggesting
It could be the perfect pet.

No hair to comb, no fur to clean,
It never needs a bath;
No need to walk it on a leash,
Or clean up in its path.

Birds are often bothersome;
Cats will scratch and shed;
Dogs will drool and bark and bite;
Hamsters must be fed.

Amoebas will do none of this;
They're clean and don't offend.
They do not mate, but duplicate
By splitting their own end.

Herring

Herring fish can travel far.
Here's some pickled in this jar!

Horseshoe Crab

To find a mate, they swim to shore
And float until they've landed.
But when the tide goes out again
Many will get stranded.

Each spring the beach is littered
With shells of those who died;
They followed nature's calling,
Abandoned by the tide.

Jellyfish

Jellyfish...oh, yuck—
A nettlesome bunch of bad luck;
A tentacled thing that carries its sting
In a mass of gelatinous muck.

The Crocodile and the Gator

A crocodile is long and sleek
And different from a gator;
Faster in the water,
His range is so much greater.

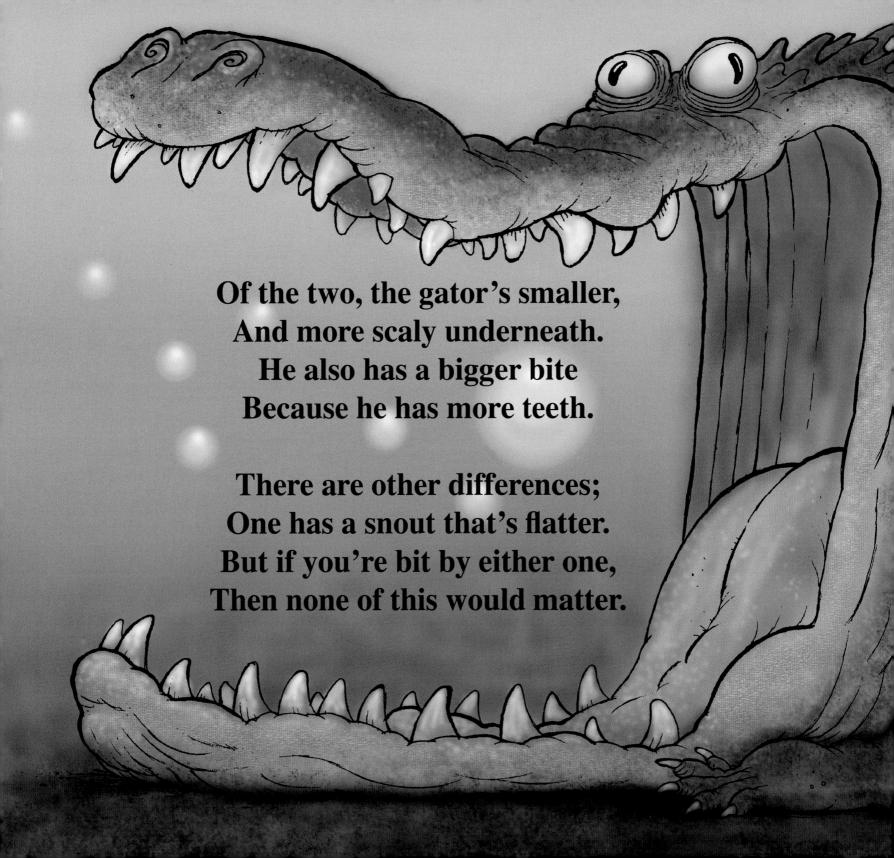

Of the two, the gator's smaller,
And more scaly underneath.
He also has a bigger bite
Because he has more teeth.

There are other differences;
One has a snout that's flatter.
But if you're bit by either one,
Then none of this would matter.

The Smallest Fish

Mirror, mirror, on the wall
Who's the smallest fish of all?
Seems the answer is complex
And varies based upon the sex.

Are we talking shortest size,
Or is it length that takes the prize?
You could measure this by weight,
But each fish is another's bait.

Barnacle

A barnacle will never fuss
Or think his life is tedious.
He likes his settled habitat,
Holding tight to where he's at.

He's often clinging to a rock,
Or on the pilings of a dock,
Happy just to bob and float,
On a big fish or a boat.

Anchored to a rusty keel,
Or on a cable made of steel,
Picks his spot and then attaches,
As he battens down his hatches.

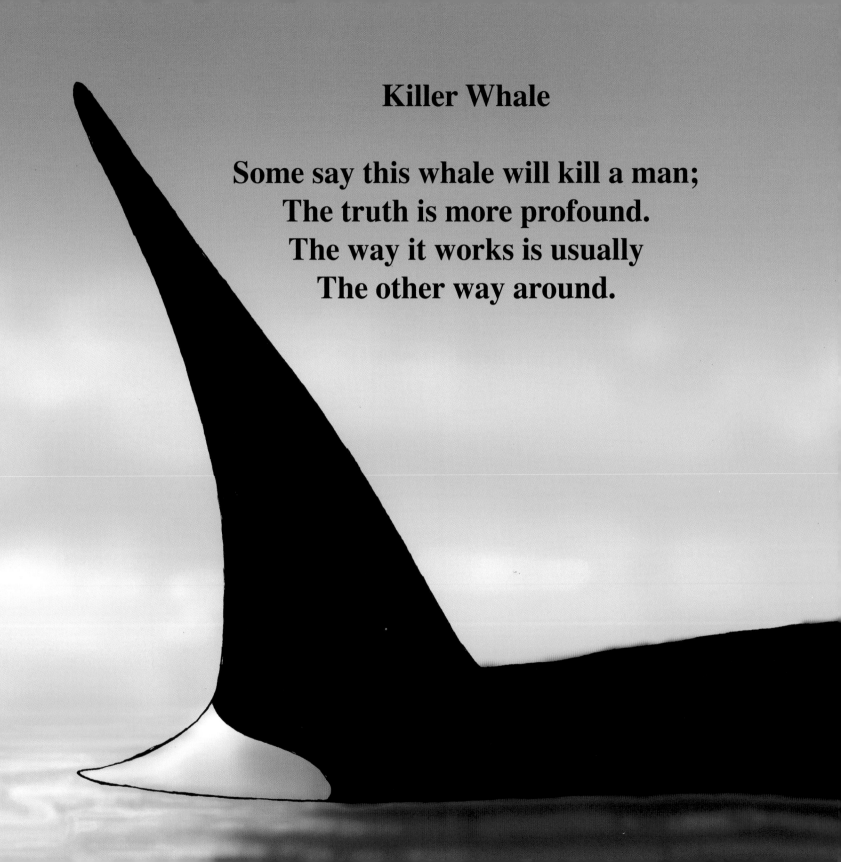

Killer Whale

Some say this whale will kill a man;
The truth is more profound.
The way it works is usually
The other way around.

Octopus

When dancing with an octopus
The movements just confound me.
For how can I move gracefully
With all those arms around me?

Puffer Fish

When you grab a puffer fish
He blows up big and wide.
So if you're near, I'd disappear!
Or simply step aside.

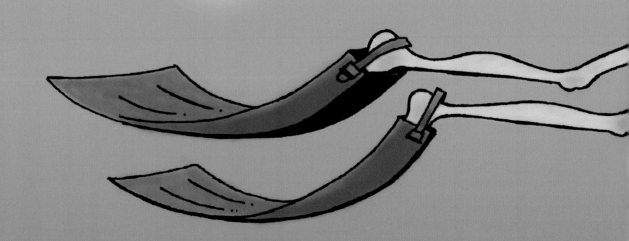

The Crab

Then there's the crab
Who complains bitterly
About how things aren't like
He wants them to be.

He's crusty, he's crass,
And also quite rude;
But if he's not careful,
He ends up as food.

Baited

Fish are always hungry
And sometimes cannot wait;
Reeled in by a shiny lure,
They'll often take the bait.

They'll latch onto a minnow,
Swimming in the brook;
Or find a worm that's squirming
On someone's fishing hook.

Sometimes snapping at a line
Will lead to pain and woe;
At times in order to survive
You have to let things go.

Pot-Bellied Seahorse

Some fathers find they often get
A bulge around the belly;
When they have kids and age a bit,
Their muscles turn to jelly.

The seahorse needs its swollen pouch
And all that body fat
To carry 'round a hundred eggs—
But I can't fathom that.

Another Pied Beauty

Glory be for spot and bass;
For trout and slug and snail;
For fresh fish swimming in the lake;
For dolphin, shark, and whale;

For scrod and scallop, smelt and shrimp;
For prawn and cod and krill;
For seaweed, sea bass, sponge, and squid;
For fin and shell and gill;

For oceans pierced with colored sails;
For people in their boats;
For lines and ropes and sunburned skin;
Praise all that swims and floats.

Sweetlips Fish are known for their large lips. They are often seen swimming alone.

Amoebas are tiny, one-celled organisms that can only be viewed with a microscope. They live in fresh water and reproduce when the cell divides into two smaller copies of itself.

Herring has been a source of food for thousands of years. There are many ways the fish is served: raw, fermented, or cured. Pickled herring is a part of many cuisines throughout the world.

Horseshoe Crabs live in shallow ocean and bay waters but come ashore to mate and often get stranded on the sand. Early horseshoe crab fossils have been found that date back 450 million years, but because of the destruction of coastal habitat and their use as bait by fishermen there has been a steady decline in their population.

Jellyfish are not really fish and not all species sting. They are found in every ocean and vary in size, shape, and color. They can be smaller than an inch or larger than seven feet in diameter with tentacles that extend more than one hundred feet. Many jellyfish sting with their tentacles, which are filled with poison that can paralyze their prey. Jellyfish found in warm-water seas have the worst stings and can be dangerous to humans.

Fish come in all sizes, shapes, and colors. They breathe through their gills, navigate by using their fins, and are unable to shut their eyes because they have no eyelids. Fish can be found in nearly all fresh and salt water environments.

Crocodiles and Alligators are different from each other. Alligators have a very broad, wide snout, while crocodiles have a narrow snout and jaw. Both alligators and crocodiles live in warm, swampy regions around the world.

Barnacles are often seen on piers and docks. They attach themselves to ships, rocks, and to other marine animals. Because they rarely move from their perches, they have developed a special way to reproduce; they have both male and female reproductive organs that allow them to fertilize themselves and produce offspring--even when there are no other barnacles nearby.

Killer Whales, also known as orcas, are mammals that are members of the dolphin family. They are found in all the oceans of the world. Killer whales are not considered a threat to humans; some feed on fish, while others hunt sea lions, seals, and walruses. Like true whales, orcas live with their mothers for their entire lives. Because females can live to be ninety years old, as many as four generations travel together and separate briefly only to mate or look for food. Some killer whale populations are now endangered due to habitat loss, oil spills, and pollution, as well as their capture for marine mammal parks.

Octopuses have four pairs of arms. They have no internal or external skeleton, allowing them to squeeze through tight places. They are intelligent and defend themselves against predators by releasing a dark, inky fluid. They travel quickly through the water, trailing their eight arms behind them as they swim. The male will live for only a few months after mating, and females die shortly after their eggs hatch. The female does not hunt during the period spent taking care of her eggs and may eat some of her own arms for sustenance. When her eggs finally hatch, the mother is often too weak to defend herself from predators. When under attack, an octopus will sometimes detach one of its arms–which can still move. The crawling arm will distract a would-be predator.

The Puffer Fish is one of the most poisonous creatures in the world, but the meat of some species is considered a delicacy in some countries. When threatened, the puffer fish will fill its stomach with water until it is many times its normal size.

Crabs are found in every ocean throughout the world. They eat dead fish and plant matter and are themselves a food source in many cultures.

Baiting is often done with worms or small fish--and sometimes with words.

The Pot-Bellied Seahorse is one of the largest species of seahorses. They have large distended bellies, and use their tails to maneuver in the water. Male seahorses become pregnant when the female deposits her eggs in the male's pouch. The male carries the eggs until they hatch, and can give birth to up to 700 babies at a time.

Another Pied Beauty is a reference to the poem "Pied Beauty" by Gerard Manley Hopkins, an English Victorian Poet.

Something Fishy © 2013 by Barry Louis Polisar Illustrations © by David Clark
Dedicated to my three Pisces --BLP
Published by Rainbow Morning Music, 2121 Fairland Road, Silver Spring, MD 20904
ISBN # 978-0-938663-53-9
First Edition, 2013